First Facts®

SCIENCE **BASICS**

WHAT IS LIGHT?

by Mark Weakland

Consultant:
Paul Ohmann
Associate Professor
College of Arts and Sciences: Physics
University of St. Thomas

PEBBLE
a capstone imprint

First Facts are published by Pebble,
1710 Roe Crest Drive, North Mankato, Minnesota 56003
www.mycapstone.com

Library of Congress Cataloging-in-Publication Data
Library of Congress Cataloging-in-Publication data is available on the Library of Congress website.
ISBN 978-1-9771-0270-6 (library binding)
ISBN 978-1-9771-0509-7 (paperback)
ISBN 978-1-9771-0275-1 (eBook PDF)

Editorial Credits
Jaclyn Jaycox and Mari Bolte, editors; Kyle Grentz, designer; Eric Gohl, media researcher; Laura Manthe, production specialist

Photo Credits
Capstone Studio: Karon Dubke, 20–21; Getty Images: Dorling Kindersley, 7; iStockphoto: Petrovich9, 19, TommL, 9; Shutterstock: Fouad A. Saad, 11, Nor Gal, 15, Piotr Krzeslak, cover, saicle, background (throughout), Stas Tolstnev, 5, udaix, 13 (top), VectorMine, 13 (bottom), Wang An Qi, 17

Printed in China.
966

TABLE OF CONTENTS

What is **Light?**

Light is all around us. It pours from the shining sun and glowing lightbulbs. We see it every time we turn on a flashlight or gaze at the moon. Light helps plants grow. Without light, nothing would be ***visible***. There is even light we can't see. We cannot touch it or hold it. So what is light, anyway?

visible—can be seen

FACT

Nothing moves faster than light in empty space. Its speed through space is 186,282 miles (300,000 kilometers) per second.

WAVES AND PARTICLES

Light can be both a wave and a ***particle***. Light travels in packets called ***photons***. Light waves can bounce off of things, like a reflection in a mirror. The waves stream through space in every direction. We cannot see most light waves.

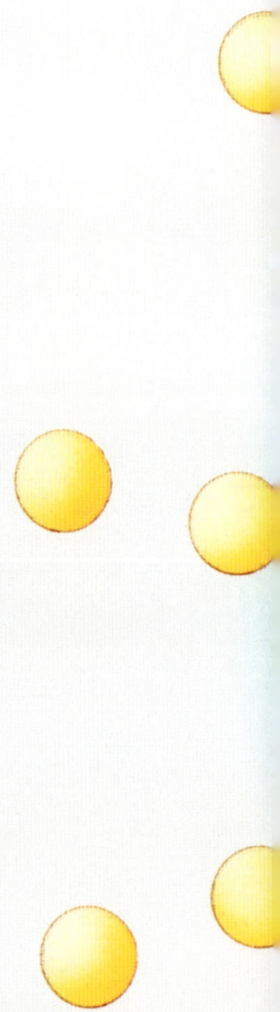

particle—a tiny piece of something
photon—a small bit of light

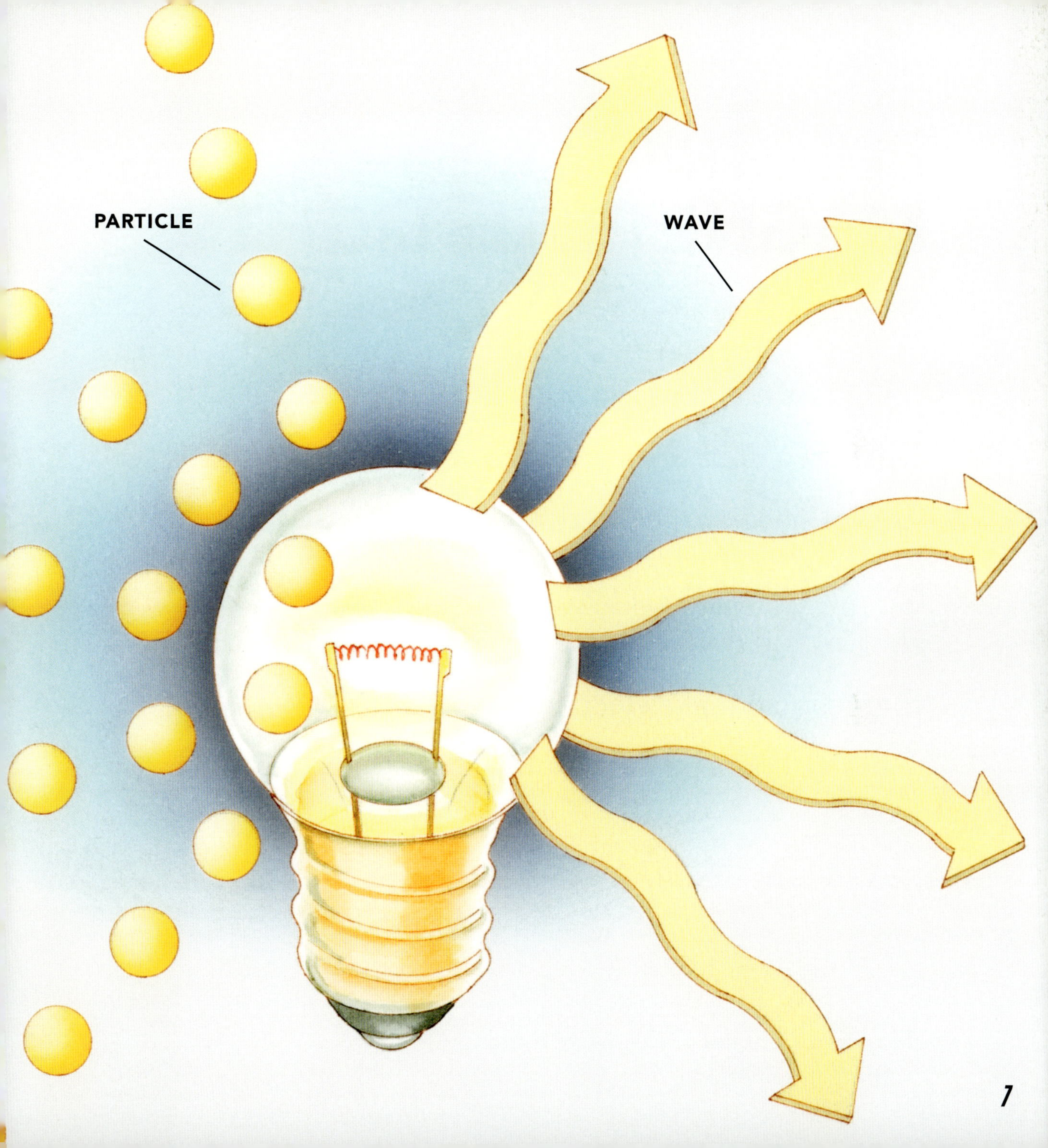
PARTICLE
WAVE

ELECTRICITY, MAGNETS, AND LIGHT

Light is made by moving ***charges***. Think of a burner on an electric stove. Charges moving through a burner make it hot, giving it a glowing red light. These same moving charges also make electricity. They make magnets push and pull.

charge—an amount of electricity running through something

LIGHT AND RADIATION

Light is a form of ***radiation***. These rays of energy spread out as they travel.

There are many types of light waves, each with its own use. Together they make the ***electromagnetic spectrum***. Visible light is only a small part of this spectrum.

radiation—rays of energy that travel out from a source

electromagnetic spectrum—the range of light that exists across the universe

A RAINBOW OF LIGHT

Light waves have different lengths and energies. With visible light, purple has the shortest wavelength. Red has the longest. When we see light, it often looks white. But white light is actually made of all the colors of the rainbow.

THE ELECTROMAGNETIC SPECTRUM

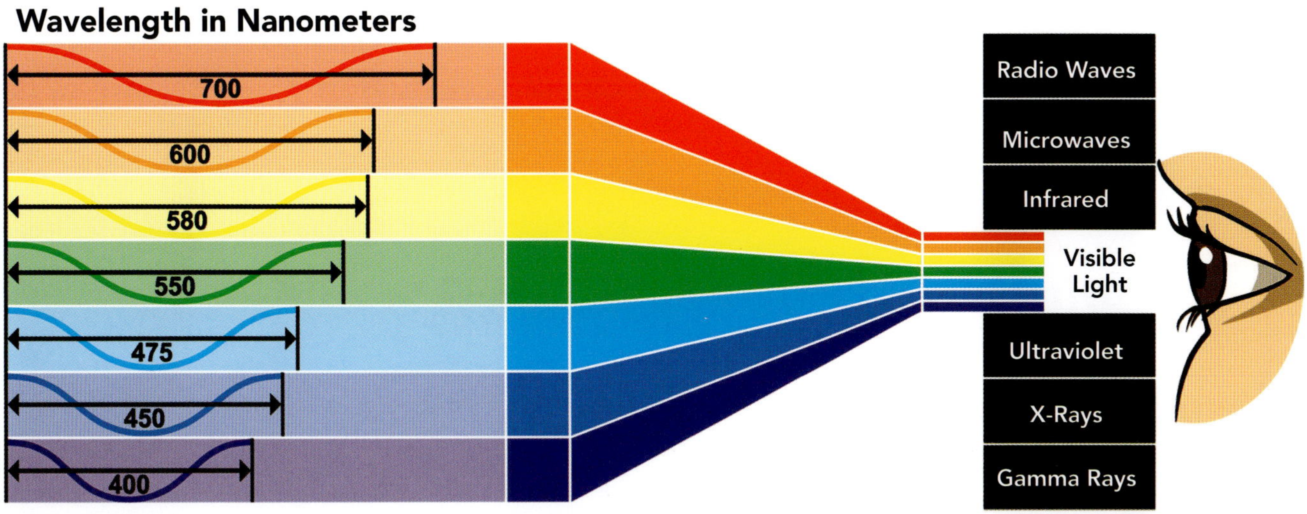

LIGHT AND WAVELENGTHS

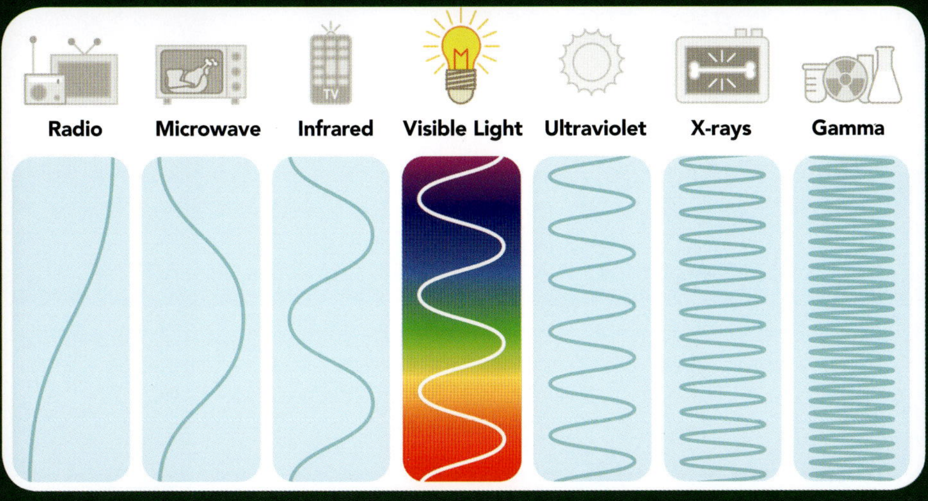

Each type of light has a different wavelength. Radio waves are long. Some measure more than a mile. Microwaves are only inches in length. Visible light wavelengths are smaller than a strand of hair. And X-rays are even shorter.

CLEANING WITH LIGHT

Ultraviolet or UV light is good at killing germs. UV light comes from the sun and from special light bulbs. Place a blanket outdoors in bright sunlight. The sunlight will kill the germs that live on it. UV light can also give us sunburns if we don't use sunscreen.

ultraviolet light—an invisible form of light that can cause sunburns

ELECTRICITY FROM SUNLIGHT

Energy from the sun's rays can be used to make electricity. ***Solar*** panels turn sunlight into electricity. Many people have solar panels on their homes. Solar energy is good for the environment. It does not produce any air pollution or harmful gases.

solar—having to do with the sun

FACT

There is a huge amount of energy in sunlight. If it could be captured, one hour of sunlight could power everything in the world for one year.

OTHER USES FOR LIGHT

Laser light is very powerful. It is used in many ways. It cuts skin during surgery. It also stitches skin back together. DVD players use light from a laser. The light reads the disk. Then a computer turns the information into pictures and sound.

"COMPUTER, TURN ON!"

Computers can turn the sound of your voice into text on a screen. A microphone receives vibrations made by your voice. It turns vibrations into small sounds a computer can read. The computer compares these sounds to a huge library of words in its memory. Then it turns the information into text.

laser—a narrow, powerful ray of light

LIGHT EXPERIMENT

USE A WATER PRISM TO EXPLORE LIGHT

MATERIALS:

- a large bowl half filled with water
- a sunny window
- a small mirror
- a sheet of white paper folded in half or in quarters

WHAT YOU DO:

1. Set the bowl on a desk near the sunny window.
2. Put the mirror in the bowl, half in and out of the water. Make sure the mirror is facing the light.
3. Hold the paper above and in front of the mirror. Move the paper until it catches the reflection from the mirror. Keep moving the paper until you see the rainbow.

WHAT HAPPENS:

The water and mirror make a prism. The prism breaks apart white light. It shows white light is made of many wavelengths. Each wavelength is seen as a different color of the rainbow.

GLOSSARY

charge (CHARJ)—an amount of electricity running through something

electromagnetic spectrum (i-lek-troh-mag-NET-ik SPEK-truhm)—the range of light that exists across the universe

laser (LAY-zur)—a narrow, powerful ray of light

particle (PAR-tuh-kuhl)—a tiny piece of something

photon (FOH-tohn)—a small bit of light

prism (PRIZ-uhm)—a transparent, triangle-shaped plastic or glass object that bends light

radiation (ray-dee-AY-shuhn)—rays of energy that travel out from a source

solar (SO-lur)—having to do with the sun

ultraviolet light (uhl-truh-VYE-uh-lit LITE)—an invisible form of light that can cause sunburns

visible (VIZH-uh-buhl)—can be seen

READ MORE

Connors, Kathleen. *Light and Color.* A Look at Physical Science. New York: Gareth Stevens Publishing, 2018.

Hansen, Grace. *Light.* Beginning Science. Minneapolis: Abdo Kids, 2018.

Mader, Jan. *How Does Light Move?* How Does It Move? Forces and Motion. New York: Cavendish Square Publishing, 2019.

INTERNET SITES

Use FactHound find Internet sites related to this book.

1. Visit *www.facthound.com*
2. Just type in 9781977102706

WWW.FACTHOUND.COM®

CRITICAL THINKING QUESTIONS

1. How can we get light from electricity?
2. Light is all around us. In what ways do we use light? Write down as many examples as you can.
3. What do you think is the most important way to use light? Use evidence from the text to support your opinion.

INDEX